50 THINGS TO KNOW ABOUT BEING AN INSTRUCTIONAL TECHNOLOGY SPECIALIST

Chellie Bankston

CZYK Publishing Since 2011.
CZYKPublishing.com
50 Things to Know

Lock Haven, PA
All rights reserved.
ISBN: 9798728462453

50 THINGS TO KNOW
BOOK SERIES
REVIEWS FROM READERS

I recently downloaded a couple of books from this series to read over the weekend thinking I would read just one or two. However, I so loved the books that I read all the six books I had downloaded in one go and ended up downloading a few more today. Written by different authors, the books offer practical advice on how you can perform or achieve certain goals in life, which in this case is how to have a better life.

The information is simple to digest and learn from, and is incredibly useful. There are also resources listed at the end of the book that you can use to get more information.

50 Things To Know To Have A Better Life: Self-Improvement Made Easy!

Author Dannii Cohen

This book is very helpful and provides simple tips on how to improve your everyday life. I found it to be useful in improving my overall attitude.

50 Things to Know For Your Mindfulness & Meditation Journey
Author Nina Edmondso

Quick read with 50 short and easy tips for what to think about before starting to homeschool.

50 Things to Know About Getting Started with Homeschool by
Author Amanda Walton

I really enjoyed the voice of the narrator, she speaks in a soothing tone. The book is a really great reminder of things we might have known we could do during stressful times, but forgot over the years.

Author Harmony Hawaii

There is so much waste in our society today. Everyone should be forced to read this book. I know I am passing it on to my family.

50 Things to Know to Downsize Your Life: How To Downsize, Organize, And Get Back to Basics

Author Lisa Rusczyk Ed. D.

Great book to get you motivated and understand why you may be losing motivation. Great for that person who wants to start getting healthy, or just for you when you need motivation while having an established workout routine.

50 Things To Know To Stick With A Workout: Motivational Tips To Start The New You Today

Author Sarah Hughes

50 THINGS TO KNOW ABOUT BEING AN INSTRUCTIONAL TECHNOLOGY SPECIALIST

BOOK DESCRIPTION

Are you considering a job as an Instructional Technology Specialist in your school? Are you considering a degree in Instructional Technology? Are you a school administrator looking for more information on the role of an Instructional Technology Specialist? If you answered yes to any of these questions then this book is for you...

50 Things to Know About Being an Instructional Technology Specialist by Chellie Bankston offers a comprehensive description of the role. Most books on instructional technology tell you about what instructional technology is and how it is used in the classroom. Although there's nothing wrong with that, what is missing is a description of what the specialist in instructional technology does day to day.

In these pages you'll discover what an Instructional Technology Specialist is, and what they are not. You'll also discover all the facets of the job and how different districts interpret the position.

By the time you finish this book, you will know about the many "hats" that Instructional Technology Specialists wear. So grab YOUR copy today. You'll be glad you did.

TABLE OF CONTENTS

DEDICATION

To all the "IT" people in education.

ABOUT THE AUTHOR

Chellie Bankston has 13 years of experience in education as both a teacher and as an Instructional Technology Specialist. She taught World History and World Geography for high school and then became an Instructional Technology Specialist where she worked at both the elementary and middle school levels. Chellie lives in Texas with her husband and four children. Currently she is working as a freelance writer, in between homeschooling, travel, and reading. Find her on Instagram, @chelliebankston.

INTRODUCTION

> *"Technology will never replace*
> *great teachers, but technology in*
> *the hands of great teachers is*
> *transformational."*

George Couros

Instructional Technology has been around for a while, but it is still new to many in education. After six years of teaching, I started thinking about what I wanted to do next. I was very sure I did not want to become a principal, but I could see that education was moving quickly towards more and more technology integration. I decided to get a graduate degree in educational technology so that I could be on the forefront of this wave of technology and help my coworkers integrate it into their curriculum. As someone who wrote curriculum for classes I was teaching and had the experience as a leader in my department, I was ready to move forward and became an Instructional Technology Specialist.

My first year was at a middle school where I was also a computer teacher, with a student teacher. I learned so much about technology that year, as well as troubleshooting, working with administrators, and teaching. I also learned how to sell teachers on instructional technology--which is something I never thought I would be able to do. I moved on to work as an Instructional Technology Specialist at an elementary school for two years. Having been a high school teacher previously, I came to have increasing respect for elementary school teachers. From there I went to work for another middle school for several years. In all of this time, I still encountered those who did not truly know what my job was.

One big thing I learned from this job is that it is not enough to integrate technology, it is never about using a computer over something else. It is about using technology tools to be, as George Couros said, to be transformational. I hope this book helps explain the role, even as it changes, and as it is different pretty much everywhere there is a school campus.

1. TITLES AND ACRONYMS FOR AN INSTRUCTIONAL TECHNOLOGY SPECIALIST

There are many titles for this position in a school setting. Often those working in the Instructional Technology Department try coming up with titles that do not end up being seen as the IT person on campus. Educational Technology Specialist/Coach, Digital Learning Specialist/Coach, Technology Instruction Specialist/Coach, Instructional Technology Specialist/Coach are all titles that various school districts have used.

In my own experience, as ITS, the S was often dropped especially with office staff who needed my assistance with IT related issues. Occasionally I run into teachers who do not understand the job either and are surprised to know that I know what I am talking about when lesson planning. I always remind them that I am just another teacher, but I am here to help now with technology integration. I try to make it apparent, but sometimes they are surprised that I taught before.

2. INSTRUCTIONAL TECHNOLOGY SPECIALISTS ARE TEACHERS FIRST

All Instructional Technology Specialists require previous teaching experience, since the job is helping teachers integrate technology into their curriculums and classrooms. I am a former history teacher, so I had lots of fun helping the Social Studies departments at my campuses. I have fun co teaching when given the opportunity.

While not all are certified in every content area, ie. Math, English, Computer Science, we all know how the technology can be built into the course or classroom. Some even co-teach with teachers to help model new technology to the students, which is especially helpful for teachers who are just getting started with technology. Teaching is the part of the job Instructional Technology Specialists often miss the most, so it's nice to be able to go into the classroom and help teach and connect with the kids.

3. SO, WHAT IS AN INSTRUCTIONAL TECHNOLOGY SPECIALIST?

Especially outside of education, people do not always know what an Instructional Technology Specialist does. Something I worked on in the past was an elevator pitch to help explain what it is. My pitch was simply--an Instructional Technology Specialist helps teachers integrate technology into their curriculum.

As educators, we know all about the lesson planning and curriculum writing process, and keep up to date with the latest technology and software. Planning with teachers and administrators we are able to help utilize technology effectively and prepare students for a world where 21st century skills are required for most jobs. That's not all we do though. Instructional Technology Specialists train teachers through professional development, teach students about how to use technologies, maintain campus equipment and databases, as well as keeping the campus website, and social media up to date. They are an important part of the campus culture and are using technology effectively for engaging content.

4. THE MANY HATS THEY WEAR

While helping teachers with enhancing curriculum is the main thing we do, in many places, the Instructional Technology Specialist is the first point of contact when technology needs troubleshooting. They can also be the person behind the campus website or social media--which is a great way to highlight the campus and be a positive part of the campus culture, and connect with students.

Other responsibilities that sometimes fall to the Instructional Technology Specialist, are things like professional development, database management, technology inventory, club leader, and computer teaching. Professional Development is a major part of the job too since teachers can learn together and benefit from dedicated time looking at technology. Sometimes that is the only way they will have the time to learn it. Managing all of the software the campus uses often entails resetting passwords for teachers or adding new teachers and students when needed. The list of 'hats' can be long, but I always prioritize time planning with teachers first.

Another hat we wear--sales. Really. There are times when I really have to sell teachers on an idea or the idea of using technology. I never thought I would be in a sales position, but sometimes, especially with more hesitant teachers, it helps.

5. COACHING ROLE

Many schools have Instructional Coaches who help with the specific content areas, so it makes sense that the Instructional Technology Specialist fulfills a coaching role when it comes to helping teachers with technology. This is why it is helpful for the Instructional Technology Specialist to be involved in teacher planning sessions. Some teachers are hesitant to use technology in the classroom and so it helps to have a "coach" there to support them when they try it for the first time.

In my own experience, I wanted to be there to see the lesson in action and to cheer on the teacher anyway. Some teachers are just fine on their own though and so checking in quickly is all they need. At times I would walk around campus during class time and just peek in and see what teachers were doing to observe which technologies were being used and how. Most teachers do not mind this, but it's important to know who you are peeking in on. I also try rewarding teachers who are using technology with badges for their classroom, which is a fun way to recognize teachers using technology. Badges can be a reward system that is visible on a classroom door or it can be something they are recognized with in other ways such as an email.

6. TROUBLESHOOTING

As stated before, many Instructional Technology Specialists are the first point of contact for troubleshooting problems--a bad printer, a computer that isn't working, a projector bulb that goes out. This is something that is learned on the job, and usually solved by calling the Information Technology department of the district. Even the Information Technology department forgets that Instructional Technology is different. I do not know how many times I was calling for a problem and had to ask them to slow down and tell me step by step. Incidentally, this role here is why the Instructional Technology Specialist is often confused for the IT guy, or girl on campus. In some districts, they might have an IT person on campus as well, but for the most part, it falls to the Instructional Technology Specialist.

A common misconception about Instructional Technology Specialists is that they know how all technology works since their title has technology in it, probably because if anyone knows how, it is the Instructional Technology Specialist. So people ask for assistance with personal items such as phones or laptops. In most districts they do not allow the Instructional Technology Specialist to work on these, since they are not district property. I always try to direct them to the right people, but mostly I have to apologize for not being able to help them in these cases.

7. COMPUTER TEACHERS WHO ALSO FULFILL THIS ROLE

In some districts, it is a computer teacher who fulfills the role of Instructional Technology Specialist in addition to their classes. Often, they don't plan with teachers, but take the responsibility of teaching digital citizenship and how-to use the computer basics to the students instead of the content teachers. They are sometimes still the first person contact for troubleshooting, social media, website, and other duties that involve the technology on campus. Often this is done in elementary and some middle schools.

I have been one of these computer teachers doing Instructional Technology, and it becomes very hard to plan with teachers this way since during planning periods you have your own classes to plan. This is where prioritizing tasks and planning is vital. Technology integration ends up being the responsibility of the teachers on their own, which in many states is a part of the teacher evaluation system in some way, shape, or form.

8. PLANNING

Planning with teachers is one of the most important aspects of the role. During teacher conference periods, personal learning conferences, before or after school, the Instructional Technology Specialist can help integrate technology by knowing what is coming up in the teachers' courses. The curriculum scope and sequence is a huge asset in planning so that the Instructional Technology

Specialist can come prepared with ideas, knowing a general idea of what is coming up. They can come up with lessons together that teach the content through the use of technology.

Not all districts have common planning periods, usually known as PLC (professional learning conferences). These are perfect however for planning with all the teachers in a specific grade and subject area at the middle and high school levels. This way everyone gets some time to plan with the Instructional Technology Specialist. I choose one day per week to plan with each subject and grade level. Usually when I attend a planning session, I participate by asking what they are currently working on and letting organic conversation create an opportunity to suggest technology.

The only issue I run into is planning with elective classes, since often they do not have a common planning period. However, they still will occasionally need assistance, so scheduling ahead of time is the key. I typically communicate with them by sending emails or checking in on them during the day.

9. RESEARCHING

Teachers do not always have time to sit and research the latest in instructional technology. The Instructional Technology Specialist stays on top of it and can also research for themselves how the technology can be used in the classroom--especially if it is a content they're not familiar with. There is a wealth of knowledge from educators who blog about their technology experiences, lesson ideas, and resources. Going to workshops and conferences also helps Instructional Technology Specialists come back to campus with fresh ideas.

With a hesitant teacher, researching something specific for them can help build trust with the Instructional Technology Specialist and then feel better about using technology later on. Sometimes all it takes is one easy piece of information to bring teachers on board with technology. Small victories are important for a hesitant teacher, so in my experience I celebrate those in a big way to encourage them to keep going. Teachers are usually very grateful for any help and praise they get.

10. SOFTWARE KNOW HOW

There are thousands of software programs out there (and apps), so of course not everyone knows how to use them. Planning is vital if new software or programs are being used, to make the new program work properly. Depending on the rules set up by the district, the Instructional Technology Specialist may have the authority to approve of the software based on criteria such as privacy standards or instructional quality. When teachers start using a new program, the Instructional Technology Specialist should go and check on how it is going, or even be there in the classroom to help out.

Several times I have been asked to help with a new program I have never seen before. However, I took the time to try to figure it out for myself to help a teacher out or direct them to the right YouTube video that helps explain it. Very often it is a matter of how much time a teacher wants to spend doing this. I always step in to help, so that teachers do not become overwhelmed by all of it and never use it again.

11. DIGITAL CITIZENSHIP

Digital Citizenship on all grade levels is an important concept for students to know. While most elementary students will not be on the internet a whole lot, there are some things they can start learning about it for databases they search, or how to navigate the school website. Especially as students become old enough for social media and more internet usage, digital citizenship is taught in every district. In some districts, teaching Digital Citizenship is done by the Instructional Technology Specialist. Sometimes, these lessons can be taught in tandem with content lessons where it fits. In some cases this means they plan a lesson and send it to teachers or teach it directly, going classroom to classroom.

In my experience, I worked with other Instructional Technology Specialists to create lessons for each grade level. We also worked on monthly lessons and slide shows for morning announcements to inform students. Where it fits, I will try to sneak it into teachers' lesson planning or let them know when good times were to mention digital citizenship.

12. VIRTUAL CLASSROOMS

Virtual teaching has become a major part of everyone's lives and so the Instructional Technology Specialist is an invaluable asset to any campus. Some teachers who may have been hesitant or lacked confidence to use technology have been thrust into technology anyway. What were previously non technology lessons have become electronic now. Teachers amidst the COVID-19 pandemic had to learn quickly how to convert to a purely electronic system. For some districts where the teachers may have been trained in how to use cloud based programs like Google Apps, or other learning management systems, they were successful at the transition, but still had to convert to a whole different way of teaching.

Learning management systems like Google Classroom, Canvas, Schoology, are great for a virtual classroom because all materials are electronic and are designed to be easy to use for both teachers and students. Instructional Technology Specialists have helped conduct online trainings through Zoom and the like to teachers, and parents to help the transition go smoothly. Creative and engaging lessons are a vital part of the system which is virtual learning.

13. SUBBING FOR PEN AND PAPER

Instructional Technology is not about swapping out pen and paper for a Chromebook. Often the Instructional Technology Specialist will work with teachers to find ways of doing something completely different, because they have a new tool to use. After all, if we can do it with pen and paper, then why switch to a computer? Students need to know how to work with technology however, because that is the world they are going to be working in when they graduate. They will need the skills learned with technology to help them in the future.

The SAMR Model (Substitution, Augmentation, Modification, Redefinition) is a good model of how technology should be integrated. Instead of using a worksheet to describe life in a different time period, students could use a simulation program to design what life looked like back then. SAMR is a good model to follow to reach a different level of instruction, however, baby steps are still recommended. If having students type a presentation using PowerPoint is where a teacher can confidently start, then celebrate and then we can work with them to reach the next level up.

14. WEBSITES AND SOCIAL MEDIA

Another common responsibility of Instructional Technology Specialists is maintaining the school website and/or social media accounts. While social media does not necessarily fall under instruction, it can be a reflection of the instruction taking place. Instructional Technology Specialists can use it to highlight instructional technology accomplishments on their campus. This is also a good way for them to have a part in the campus culture, by taking pictures of various school events and promoting them through social media.

I myself maintained social media on the campuses I worked for. Typically I used the various social media accounts for different reasons. Twitter was a way to promote our campus to the district, Instagram was mainly to connect campus happenings with the students, and Facebook was really to disseminate information to parents and community members. The website updates that I do are usually staff directory updates and announcements on the homepage. Every district is different and may have others working on the website or social media.

15. QUALITY SOFTWARE, SUBSCRIPTIONS, APPS, AND PROGRAMS

Occasionally, a teacher will come to an Instructional Technology Specialist with a new program, app, or website they found. A good first step is for them both to look at the product and decide its quality--does it meet the district's standards for education, and does it meet the district's standards for privacy? If it does not, then the Instructional Technology Specialist can help find an alternative. Many districts will have a process for teachers to go through for approval on new programs, so the Instructional Technology Specialist is a good person to start with.

Some districts are stricter than others about programs, but in my experience, having a solid process for vetting programs is important, so that there are good, quality choices for teachers to choose from.

16. CURRICULUM AND LESSON PLANS

Because they have previous teaching experience, Instructional Technology Specialists know how to write a good lesson plan. When working with teachers, we help them come up with ways to use their existing technology to create great lessons to enhance the curriculum, and engage the students. This is why planning time with teachers is so important, however, if it is not possible in some districts, the Instructional Technology Specialist will send ideas out in emails.

At times, my part in planning was the 'idea' person. I came up with or borrowed ideas from others and suggested them to teachers while they were planning. Sometimes though, there is not time for this, and I end up sending an email with my suggestions instead and sometimes I get a response,

and sometimes not, but I do follow up with teachers
later to see what they thought of the idea.

17. DAY TO DAY

The day to day activities of an Instructional
Technology Specialist will differ based on a number
of activities. One day may be all planning day with
teachers, while others may be in the classroom co-
teaching or observing. Instructional Technology
Specialists will also do their administrative tasks--
depending on which ones they are responsible for--
website, inventory, troubleshooting, researching,
planning professional development or a lesson idea,
etc. There is rarely a boring day in this job.

I keep up with all my day to day activities on my
Google calendar. Even if it is just a few minutes with
a teacher or administrator in a hallway, I mark it
down. Meeting in the hallway happens more often
than people think. In my experience, walking down
hallways meant I was stopped a couple of times for
questions before reaching my destination. However, a
calendar helps keep track of everything I need to do,
but also provides others with an idea of what an

Instructional Technology Specialist does all day (and reminds them how valuable they are).

18. WORKING WITH ADMINISTRATORS

Most Instructional Technology Specialists work closely with the school principal for purchasing, professional development, website content, and other planning decisions. The principal drives the instructional decisions on campus, so they will have the final say on the aforementioned activities. Open communication is vital to successful instructional technology usage on campus. Typically, as long as there is evidence that the technology is tied to the district standards and that it is engaging to the students and making them successful, administrators will support the Instructional Technology Specialist.

Administrators are typically very busy people and often pulled in various directions. I have found that I can get quick answers to questions walking down the hall with a principal who is on their way somewhere, instead of waiting for them to answer an email or be in their office. However, I have also had principals who are on top of their emails.

19. EVENING EVENTS

Schools often have evening events to showcase their academics to parents and the community. Sometimes the Instructional Technology Specialist can use one of these events to showcase the exciting lessons students are doing with technology. This could be a STEM event, or just an Academic Night where each subject area showcases a technology inspired lesson they are working on.

As an Instructional Technology Specialist on an elementary level, I participated in academic nights by helping teacher teams come up with games or activities that included technology components. On the middle school level, I was a part of academic nights where I took pictures of kids in front of the green screen, but also had booths set up with various technologies people could play with like Ozobots or software programs open on computers.

20. SCHOOL CLUBS

One way for an Instructional Technology Specialist to be involved in the campus and connect with students, is hosting a club if that is an option in the school. Makerspaces, STEM Clubs, Computer Coding, or Audio/Visual Clubs are just some of the various clubs they could lead. Often the Instructional Technology Specialist can find curriculums, software, or ideas to use in the various clubs.

In my experience I hosted a technology club where students learned some basic troubleshooting solutions that they were able to help their teachers out with in a bind, like switching between modes on the projector display, or where to go when a program would freeze up. I also hosted the broadcast club where students recorded a morning news show for the campus. These are great ways to connect with students, especially when missing the teaching aspect of being in the classroom.

21. PROFESSIONAL DEVELOPMENT FOR TEACHERS

Since a major part of the job is helping teachers integrate technology into the curriculum, professional development is a great way to introduce new ideas to teachers. Training time also gives teachers time, not only to think of how they are going to use the information, but actually plan out their lessons. Planning a professional development is a good avenue for helping a teacher struggling with incorporating technology as well. Professional development should however, be connected to school initiatives and needs based on district surveys or other provided information.

Standing up in front of an adult audience was once a terrifying prospect, however leading teachers in professional development became one of my favorite parts of being an Instructional Technology Specialist. Since missing the interaction of a classroom is a common aspect of teaching that people in this position miss the most, being able to see the light bulbs go on in adult students is just as special. Professional development trainings can be on anything either productivity related--how to use or organize files on the computer, or instruction related.

22. THE BEGINNING OF THE SCHOOL YEAR

The beginning of the school year can be hectic. Instructional Technology Specialists typically are making sure teachers have the equipment they need, onboarding new teachers, making sure student equipment is ready to go, updating the website for the new school year, and planning out how best to plan with teachers. This time of year is usually filled with meetings with administrators for planning purposes, training from the Instructional Technology department for the specialists, and creating professional development training for teachers.

I usually spent some serious time allocating computer carts to teachers since at the time, we had one cart per two teachers at the district I worked at. Updating the website with new staff and removing old staff, planning out my schedule of teacher planning periods were some of the other activities I did to prepare for the year. I also start the year with a few goals to work toward and how to accomplish them.

23. THE END OF THE SCHOOL YEAR

The end of the year is a great time for reflection on the whole year--what worked, what did not, etc. I keep notes all year so that I know what to go back to at the end of the year. One issue I kept having was disappearing audio cords, which meant more purchasing. I came up with a better system for the next year to make sure audio cords returned. This is also the time of year when teachers are returning equipment for the summer, and Instructional Technology Specialists usually have a part in the teacher checkout process. The end of the year is also a good time to organize some inventory, check on the status of student equipment and other instructional technology devices.

I found myself going room to room to see if any technology was left out in the classrooms, clearing off photos from ipads, and taking inventory of student laptop carts at this time of year. A spreadsheet of all the check out items for teachers was immensely helpful in keeping track of everything, so that at the beginning of the year, it was all accounted for. I also spent time cleaning screens, keyboards, and other equipment.

24. ELEMENTARY SCHOOL

Every level of education is different in terms of Instructional Technology and elementary schools are no exception. Elementary teachers teach multiple subjects a day, so their planning time is precious. For the Instructional Technology Specialist, researching and helping with planning specific lessons is crucial to success. Support in the classroom is helpful, especially with the younger children, when getting started with new technology. Younger students often need more direction and help with logging in to various programs. Often the lesson plans that I helped with on this level included support for reading skills, so at the kindergarten level, students spent time learning the letters on the keyboard. With the older students we learned how to write emails.

In some places students have dedicated Computer class as a part of their rotations between PE, Music, and Art classes. If once a week is all the students get, it can be hard to build a foundation of computer basics with them, but there are programs that help teach them basics. Often on this level the computer teacher ends up being the 'technology' person on campus anyway, so they will be the one maintaining websites and social media, and be responsible for teaching students these computer basics.

25. MIDDLE SCHOOL

People have often said that it takes a special person to work at a middle school, considering the age group of the students. Joking aside, instructional technology at the middle school level can be a little more advanced at this level, students start learning more about technology through pre-engineering courses or other computer courses, which means they can learn using more technology. Digital Citizenship at this level takes on a new meaning as students are using computers and the internet more often starting in middle schools.

Instructional Technology Specialists at this level usually have more opportunities with teachers at this level since in many districts they have two planning periods. In my experience on this level, I met once a week during the common planning period with teachers and spent time in their classrooms as well.

26. HIGH SCHOOL

At a high school, there are many more teachers to support, so some high schools may be lucky and have more than one Instructional Technology Specialist. This may make it hard for them to co teach with teachers, but planning with teachers still occurs and is very important. High School may also prove to be slightly more difficult where an Instructional Technology Specialist may not be familiar with a content. However, they can still offer general ideas that can fit into any content. I myself taught high school, and if I ever went back, there are plenty of ideas I could use to teach my content---like virtual trips, simulations, games, presentations, etc.

On this level, the students can be more involved in the care of their equipment and in some places they might have a student club where they can learn general troubleshooting to help their peers. This may be something that the Instructional Technology Specialist might supervise.

27. COLLEGE LEVEL

Instructional Technology on a college campus will look a lot different. Instead of planning with teachers and incorporating technology into the curriculum, it is more about teaching the instructors how to use technology to teach. The Instructional Technology Specialist may be asked to give webinars or seminars on technology for the classroom or for multimedia presentations. They will also work with students through learning management systems to get them acclimated with the technology.

With a multitude of online college courses, learning management systems like Blackboard and Canvas are commonplace. Instructional Technology Specialists at this level usually have experience with managing the back end of these systems with account creation, etc. and helping students and professors become familiar with them through training or documents with instructions.

28. TECHNOLOGY OVERLOAD

There is so much going on in the world of instructional technology, it is easy to become overwhelmed by it. Everything is better in moderation, as the old adage states. When training teachers about new programs or hardware in instructional technology, it's helpful to focus on one thing at a time and learn it well, before moving on to the next big idea. Especially with teachers who are hesitant to try new technology, it is helpful to be in the classroom for support and start with something small.

There is also nothing wrong with becoming an expert with something that works. Kahoot and Quizizz are both competitive quiz programs. Just because a new version of something else comes out, does not mean it is time to move on. Besides that, some of those programs will have updates that catch up with the times later on.

29. TEACHERS AND THEN EVERYONE ELSE

For many Instructional Technology Specialists, they are first contact for any technology issues that arise on campus. Sometimes, this means running to the front office because a printer is not online, or to the auditorium when the sound is not working properly. While most will go and help out where they can, their first duty is to teachers and their curriculum.

As an Instructional Technology Specialist myself, I have not had any problems helping everyone unless I was co teaching in a classroom. In those moments, if it was not an emergency, I simply waited until I was available to go and help. Half the time, I would get to the emergency and they had figured it out by then.

30. WHAT COUNTS AS INSTRUCTIONAL TECHNOLOGY

If it plugs in it counts as instructional technology, right? No, instructional technology is technology used to enhance instruction. So the classroom phone or the auditorium sound system are not usually going to be under an Instructional Technology Specialist's purview. The Instructional Technology Specialist is first, an education specialist. However, we are often called to be troubleshooters in those cases though. Those are "foot in the door" opportunities to pop in and observe what technology is being used in the classroom and how. Often, it is an opportunity to come back later and discuss ideas. I have been several times in a classroom for one task and then asked to help them with a class activity.

31. INSTRUCTIONAL TECHNOLOGY AND SCHOOL LIBRARIANS

Gone are the days of the school librarian who only recommends books and teaches the Dewey Decimal system. Librarians these days work closely with the Instructional Technology Specialists for media resources and creative ways to approach library classroom lessons. In some special cases, a librarian will also be the Instructional Technology Specialist since they check certain equipment out to teachers, however, this would be a tremendous amount of work on a librarian. The Instructional Technology Specialist and the school librarian can make a great team though, especially for collaborations where technology and research through electronic media is used.

In my time, I have worked with several librarians and we have collaborated on professional development activities, check in/out procedures, as well as library lessons with technology. Another collaborative effort between librarians and this position is makerspaces. Makerspaces have become a trend in the past few years. Basically, it is a space (often times in the library) where students can make anything--typically something related to STEM, but it can be anything. Some makerspaces have cards with challenges on them, but some will have just materials and space to work. Since there is technology involved with some of these activities, an Instructional Technology Specialist may be called on to help monitor a makerspace, as well as the librarian since it is usually a space within the library.

32. KEEPING UP WITH TEACHING CERTIFICATIONS

In most cases, Instructional Technology Specialists have a teaching certification. They can keep up their certification hours through their own professional development activities and meetings they attend. Going to conferences and workshops are great ways to keep up hours for certifications especially since they are directed at teachers most often and so they are still practicing their educator skill set. Of course various states have differing rules about certifications and keeping them up to date, so it is best to look them up.

33. INSTRUCTIONAL VS. INFORMATION

The Instructional Technology Specialist is often confused for IT. While in some places the two departments may work closely together at times, Instructional Technology is about using the technology to enhance curriculum. Information Technologists are the ones maintaining the equipment and programs.

Because the Instructional Technology Specialist does some troubleshooting on campus, the two departments will keep in close contact. In my experience, I had the IT department number memorized because I was on the phone with them so often. Usually if it is something I do not know how to solve within a few minutes, I called them and they were typically able to help over the phone. There is definitely a learning curve with this part of the job, but as the old saying goes, you learn something new everyday.

34. STANDARDIZED TESTING DATA AND OTHER DATA SOURCES

Standardized testing in schools has an effect on everything, including instructional technology. Test scores can drive curriculum, so any instructional technology planning that addresses gaps in learning according to this data, is helpful to teachers and the campus. When administration and teachers can see how instructional technology is beneficial to students and drives up learning, they are more likely to be open to technology initiatives. We do not use technology for the sake of using technology--which is a misconception about instructional technology in general, that it is just for fun and engaging activities. We use technology to enhance the curriculum, teach 21st century skills, and learn in a new way. For the Instructional Technology Specialist, testing data can provide an idea of which skills students are lacking and how a technology lesson may be beneficial to the students. Bringing this data to planning sessions is important. I reference the data and use it to help guide my own planning of technology ideas. Students need more work in reading comprehension, so my technology lessons address those issues.

Other data sources may be climate surveys or district surveys that give students, staff, and parents an opportunity to answer questions. This data can give an Instructional Technology Specialist an idea about how technology is used on campus, how the different groups perceive it, how much support they get in the classroom, and concerns parents may have about it. I often use this information and information from technology surveys to guide the trainings I plan for professional development.

35. HESITANT TEACHERS

Some teachers, young and old, are just hesitant to use technology. Whether they do not feel they are up to the task, or do not see the benefit, Instructional Technology Specialists are there to support them and help them take baby steps. Showing hesitant teachers the benefit while in the planning stages is vital so that the teacher sees what can happen when students are given 21st century tools. For some teachers, it's about having someone there if something goes wrong during a lesson. Building trust is important especially with these teachers.

I tried to encourage teachers to do lessons that started with a small, easy project that students could do and then celebrate the small victories. Teachers sometimes learn that their students know what to do with technology more often than they think. Teachers then start feeling more confident with technology and will then take some bigger leaps. Often I will clear my schedule for a teacher just starting with technology so that I am available if something happens and they are not sure what to do.

36. BUILDING RELATIONSHIPS YEAR ONE

The first year on a new campus for anyone in this position is about building trust and relationships. While some teachers will jump right in and go, others take time to get to know the Instructional Technology Specialist before trusting that they can depend on them. This is why it is so important for the Instructional Technology Specialist to be visible and to be part of teacher planning meetings, staff meetings, and other events on campus.

I've been on a few campuses and year one is always the getting to know you year. I find that the beginning of the year meetings and staff development are good ways to get to know the staff as a whole. As the year gets started, attending planning meetings from the beginning are beneficial in setting a standard that the Instructional Technology Specialist is going to be a regular attendee at the meetings. This helps build a foundation for future planning.

37. THE NEXT STEP YEAR TWO

By the second year on campus, Instructional Technology Specialists know their campus pretty well. Teachers know them and how they can be a great resource, and are less hesitant since there is a level of trust built from the first year. Planning comes easier as teachers know the Instructional Technology Specialist, so it is this year that they can start new projects on campus, such as training everyone to be Google Educator Certified, or Hour of Code lessons, etc. The second year is a little easier than the first, but is still a building year as everyone is still learning about each other.

I found in my second year on campus that teachers were more apt to call me for help and use me as a resource for planning purposes. I had my procedural systems in place that worked the previous year and was able to tweak the ones that did not. The second year is the year I really start pushing teachers to take their technology integration to the next level--which is different for each teacher, but we use forward thinking. Instructional Technology Specialists can make goals for the second year and by now they have a good sense of where the campus is and where they are headed.

38. MULTIPLE CAMPUSES

Some Instructional Technology Specialists will cover multiple campuses. This happens when budgets are short or it's a small district where it can be managed. Managing two or more campuses is challenging, especially for planning purposes when an Instructional Technology Specialist is intending to be in a teacher's classroom. However, scheduling ahead of time, planning far in advance with teachers, and working with administration to create a system can help alleviate the stress of multiple campuses.

In my experience as an Instructional Technology Specialist, I covered someone else's campus while they were out. It takes planning and working with two administrators, but it can be done. In some districts there may only be one person who covers all campuses on one level, so they make it work the best they can. Sometimes it means they are only on campus one or two days per week.

39. A WEEKLY NEWSLETTER

A great way for Instructional Technology Specialists to disseminate information to teachers is through an email newsletter. A weekly newsletter can be a source of announcements for training or campus happenings, or to introduce quick tips and tricks, or to provide resources for other technology ideas teachers may have. One idea for newsletters is to ask a question that teachers can respond to, to show that they've read it. Other ideas to include in newsletters is recognition of teachers who have done technology lessons so that other teachers--maybe the hesitant ones--can see that technology does have a place in the classroom.

I put my newsletters out on a Google Slides presentation so that everyone can see the previous weeks' newsletters. Included on these newsletters, I place links to resources as well. I mention procedural announcements, recognize teachers who are integrating technology well, and provide tips and tricks for the week. This is also something that in my experience was a collaborative effort. Other Instructional Technology Specialists in the district collaborated on newsletters and sent those out to their campuses. This provided some consistency throughout the district.

40. FOOT IN THE DOOR

Sometimes Instructional Technology Specialists can get the proverbial foot in the door with teachers by popping in when they need technical help. By observing the lesson as they fix tech issues, they can later make comments or suggestions for how technology could enhance their lesson. Simply by being seen is a great first step to let teachers know that they are a resource that can help out with instruction.

I have done this many times. I have been in for a technical issue or even just to pop in and observe and am able to make some mental notes about how I can help the teacher with how to integrate technology in a lesson. Sometimes this is the best way to sell a teacher on an idea when they may have been hesitant before.

41. ISLAND OF ONE

Sometimes it is easy for an Instructional Technology Specialist to feel like an island of one on campus, so it is important to be involved on campus in other ways. Help with morning duty, chaperone an event, attend social gatherings, etc. to be a part of the campus are great ways to get involved. Also helpful is building a network with other district Instructional Technology Specialists so that they have support for their specific job challenges and obstacles. Instructional Technology Specialists also have job commonalities with Instructional Coaches that are sometimes on campus. Another way to avoid this feeling is to be out of the office.

Campuses will often have committees to participate in as the Instructional Technology Specialist--leadership committees, district level committees, and/or technology committees on campus. These committees are important for the Instructional Technology Specialist to be a part of, so that instructional technology is not lost in the campus or district. An advocate for instructional technology is a wise asset to these committees to promote technology usage in the correct ways.

One of the ways Instructional Technology Specialists can be visible and accessible to staff, thereby getting out of the office, is working from a common area that teachers will be crossing through. I often worked from the library, when it was not disruptive to classes, so that teachers would be able to talk with me when they were crossing through or bringing classes into the library. I also always leave a note on my office door to know where to find me, in case there is someone looking for me.

42. ON THE RESUME

A resume for an Instructional Technology Specialist will no doubt have their previous education experience on it. The resume should point out the qualities that would make them a good Instructional Technology Specialist--someone who is self motivated, but also a team player, someone who can teach both students, and adults, someone who is a leader, and someone who is up to date with technology lessons and how they might be used across curriculums. Instructional Technology Specialists can be any educator from computer teacher to history teacher. I have a master's degree in educational technology, but this is not always a prerequisite.

As a part of my resume, I included an online portfolio of my accomplishments as a teacher, and provided multiple examples of lessons where I used technology to enhance my curriculum.

43. IDEAS FOR THE COMPUTER TECHNOLOGY CLASSROOM

It seems like the computer technology teacher would be in good shape since their content is all computer based. However, there are still things they can do differently to add a layer of technology. Perhaps they can change a lesson on writing a resume, to include components such as a video resume or adding a picture profile and graphic design to it. Depending on the content of the course, teachers can still modify old lessons and use the Instructional Technology Specialist as a resource.

There are certainly many different computer courses that students take. I proposed to a middle school level technology applications class, to have students help me with our campus website. Students were tasked with coming up with a graphic design for various events happening on campus, and their work would be used for the website. In a yearbook class, students created advertisements both graphics and videos for selling the yearbook.

44. IDEAS FOR THE SOCIAL STUDIES CLASSROOM

History and Geography are not all memorizing dates and finding places on a map. Simulations can be an engaging way of learning more about history. Virtual 3D field trips are a fun way to experience different places students have not been before. Creating maps with software or creating a video presentation of historical events especially exciting in a Social Studies classroom.

Virtual field trips are especially exciting for history, to set the scene of historical events. I had world culture students viewing various places, which helped them connect with the history and culture of the region they were studying. Students also had fun creating puppet shows with a green screen and ipad to study a new culture. They researched their cultures and created a skit that they performed in front of a green screen and recorded with the ipad.

45. IDEAS FOR THE SCIENCE CLASSROOM

Instructional Technology can easily accommodate a STEM class. While using hands on materials, students can record a video of their process. Students can design models of projects using a 3D printer--for example a molecule or a model of layers of the earth. There are many apps that students can use to keep track of experiments, create simulations, or participate in a safe virtual lab.

One of my favorite lessons was using the ipads to create stop animation. Students in one class worked in groups to create models of pangea drifting into continents and in another class they modeled kinetic and potential energy drawing out roller coasters and showing how each energy worked.

46. IDEAS FOR THE MATH CLASSROOM

The best way to learn something is to teach it. So, having students create their own videos on how to work out a math problem is beneficial in showing the student's process and understanding of a problem. A lesson that I proposed to math classes was having students create a stop animation video of how to do a math problem and sharing it with the class. Another idea for a math lesson is using various applications for puzzles and logic, graphing calculators, or manipulatives.

47. IDEAS FOR THE ENGLISH LANGUAGE ARTS CLASSROOM

With so many facets to the English language and literature, there are several ways to incorporate instructional technology for this content. Write a commercial and create a video, use a slide presentation to write individual paragraphs of an essay with editing tools, or practice typing skills while typing out research are just a few of the ways English teachers can incorporate technology on a basic level. Using technology for research is definitely a good skill to learn considering the mass amount of information available to students. There is also software that helps students who are struggling readers with vocabulary, and also help with highlighted text, and other tools to help readers.

Students in a 7th grade course were studying A Christmas Carol, and so I had them do a virtual field trip with 3D viewers of Charles Dickens' home and London at the time, to help set the scene for them as they read. One 21st Century skill that I suggest to teachers is having students type their papers, which helps the students practice typing skills while also learning writing.

48. FINE ARTS CLASSES AND TECHNOLOGY

Music, Theatre, Art classes? Of course instructional technology can help in all of these places, I found that tablets were versatile in these classes. In art classes, students can use art concepts to design a project for the 3D printer. There are overwhelming amounts of art apps students can use to draw in different mediums. Students can learn graphic design concepts as well and create posters for events on campus.

Tablets with apps for reading music or scripts where students can make annotations are helpful in music and theatre classes. Music students can learn how to make music with technology. In elementary music classes, students were able to use ipads to practice various instruments that they did not have on hand in the school and come up with music as a class. For middle and high school performing arts music classes, often they annotate their music on the tablets and practice with various music tools. Theatre classes use technology for annotating scripts or recording their acting to self critique.

49. UPWARD MOBILITY

Where does an Instructional Technology Specialist promote to? Of course there are administrator positions in the department itself at the district level. Depending on the district it may require leadership experience such as on a campus level as an assistant or head principal. With the leadership experience in the job itself on top of curriculum and coaching experience, there are lateral moves like curriculum coach that Instructional Technology Specialists can do as well. After that it is up to the district, but there is definitely opportunity for advancement in this type of position.

50. WHAT AN INSTRUCTIONAL TECHNOLOGY SPECIALIST CAN LEARN

What skills does an Instructional Technology Specialist learn that can be beneficial in the future? Coaching teachers and training adults through planning with teachers, providing professional development, and serving on campus committees are skills that they will learn through this job. An Instructional Technology Specialist also learns leadership as they are the technology leader on campus and most likely given other responsibilities that teachers would not necessarily have. While on the job they also learn much about technology and how it works, and how to troubleshoot at the same time. Some decide to go back to the classroom and teach, bringing with them a wealth of knowledge of how to incorporate technology and many ways they can use it to be transformational teachers. They go on to be leaders no matter where they go in education.

OTHER HELPFUL RESOURCES

International Society for Technology in Education
https://www.iste.org/

Learn about Technology Integration
https://www.edutopia.org/technology-integration

National Education Technology Plan
https://tech.ed.gov/netp/

READ OTHER
50 THINGS TO KNOW
BOOKS

50 Things to Know

Stay up to date with new releases on Amazon:

https://amzn.to/2VPNGr7

CZYKPublishing.com

50 Things to Know

We'd love to hear what you think about our content! Please leave your honest review of this book on Amazon and Goodreads. We appreciate your positive and constructive feedback. Thank you.